MALALA
Poems for Malala Yousafzai

A GOOD WORKS PROJECT

All proceeds from the sale of this book are donated
to the Malala Fund (www.malalafund.org)

MALALA
Poems for Malala Yousafzai

Edited by
Joseph Hutchison & Andrea L. Watson

FUTURECYCLE PRESS
www.futurecycle.org

Published by FutureCycle Press
Hayesville, North Carolina, USA

ISBN 978-1-938853-36-4

all for Malala

CONTENTS

Foreword

Late on Tuesday, October 9, 2012, I read the news that a group of Taliban gunmen wearing masks had stormed onto a bus in Pakistan and shot a 15-year-old girl in the head, wounding two others as well. The targeted victim was Malala Yousafzai, who had outraged the Taliban by taking to the blogosphere to advocate for the rights of women, especially for the right of girls in her region to an education. She had been speaking out since the age of 11, and the fundamentalists had decided it was time to silence her. *The New York Times* reported that a bullet was lodged in Malala's brain, and it was unclear if she would survive—or, if she survived, what her quality of life might be going forward.

Like most people, I was heart-sickened by the Taliban's act, and being a poet I had no choice but to get my reaction down in words. But the small poem that flowed onto my notebook page surprised me: Instead of anguish or raw dismay, it expressed admiration for Malala's courage and a conviction that her example would survive, even if she herself might not. I decided to post my poem on my blog without changing a word, less as an example of great poetry than as a cry in the dark.

When I logged on to my computer to post the poem, a notice popped up that a fellow blogger, the Canadian poet and critic Conrad DiDiodato (an early riser), had already posted a poetic response to the news about Malala in the form of a haiku. I read it and liked it so much that I decided to tinker slightly with my poem so that, like his, it directly addressed Malala. Then I posted my poem and a snippet from and a link to *The New York Times* article, pointed my readers to Conrad's poem on his blog, and ended the post with this offhand remark: "Perhaps we need a worldwide garland of poems beginning with 'Malala....'"

Within the hour I received an email from Diane Kistner, Director of FutureCycle Press, offering to produce an anthology of poems honoring the life and vision of Malala Yousafzai with all of the proceeds donated to an appropriate charitable organization in Malala's name. The anthology would become one of the press's Good Works projects, "issue-oriented anthologies of work designed to increase awareness and help make our world a better place." After a few weeks of hectic discussion and planning, Diane tapped me and poet/editor Andrea L. Watson to edit the collection.

As word got out about the project, submissions began to come in from poets all over the world. Many more heartfelt poems were submitted to us than we could possibly include in the anthology, but we read every one of them. Many poets included letters of support for Malala, expressing a sense of deep concern, connection, and love— yes, love—for her. Clearly, this brave young woman had stirred the voices in all of us to rise up and be heard.

Now, a fast-paced year later, *Malala: Poems for Malala Yousafzai* is complete. It begins with the two "seed poems" from which it grew— Conrad's and my own—and spirals out in beautiful and unexpected ways to touch, through the imaginations of scores of poets, on the meaning of Malala's message. It is first, of course, a message of suffering and survival; but more, it is a message of courage, commitment, and freedom of the mind and spirit.

***

Anyone who saw Malala speak before the United Nations on her sixteenth birthday—July 12, 2013, declared by U.N. Secretary-General Ban Ki-moon and the United Nations as "Malala Day"—knows how powerful and inspiring her message is. "Dear sisters and brothers," she addressed us all, and the world found it impossible not to listen to her clear, determined voice. Rather than lament the evil that had been done to her, Malala expressed confidence in the justice of her goals and focused her gaze firmly on a future in which governments "ensure freedom and equality for women so that they can flourish." Simply and elegantly, Malala expressed what all of us know but too easily forget: "One child, one teacher, one book and one pen can change the world."

Is it possible, too, that one poet, one pen, and one poem can change the world? Has not history already answered that question for us? In a cultural sense, poets have traditionally been "first responders," although the current bias in the West is against poetry that speaks from an ideologically engaged position. In fact, cultural arbiters—academia, arts organizations, grant-making foundations, and the vast majority of publishers—prefer to foster the careers of poets who adopt strictly personal and/or theoretical stances in their work.

These arbiters especially devalue public poetry. Hence the outrage when, in 1968, Robert Bly not only won the National Book Award for his deeply political *The Light Around the Body* but publicly turned over his award money to an activist group opposed to the Vietnam War. And when Sam Hamill edited and published an anthology of poems against the Second Gulf War, the collection was widely condemned by reviewers, many of whom declared poetry unsuitable for political expression. In the past few years, poets called upon to write public poems for presidential inaugurations have been widely mocked —often not for writing poorly, but for attempting to address public concerns at all.

Why should poets be denied the kind of intimate public address we heard from Malala? Why should poets not be free to respond to events outside the narrow confines of their own neighborhoods and their customary poetics?

***

This anthology is evidence that some poets still dare to respond to what's happening in the larger world, and we believe they are making a significant contribution in doing so. They demonstrate that poetry can have a real-world effect—that writing poems need not be just an academic exercise or a means of advancing one's "literary career." With *Malala,* poets are helping to raise awareness about the oppression of women. Perhaps they can also raise some money to help educate girls and relegate their oppression to the past.

Of course, nobody thinks that poetry alone can end oppression any more than it has ever ended a war, but it can push readers to think beyond their personal concerns. Maybe, in the process, it can help them understand that the cause of a child crying out for intellectual freedom in a foreign country is their own cause, too.

—Joseph Hutchison

My parents believed that everything was possible for their daughter.

Hold your head up high and walk into the future.

At a women's college, whose strong liberal arts curriculum stressed intellect, profession, and community, I quickly came to appreciate the camaraderie of like minds learning and living together. Years later, teaching at St. Mary's Academy, in Colorado, one of the oldest college preparatory high schools for young women in the United States, how wonderful it was to once again find and foster that same vision—women attaining their power through education.

Somehow, I took that endless horizon of choices—in education, family, and career—for granted. If everything were possible for women in the twentieth and twenty-first centuries, would it not be so across pockets of distant valleys, pathways leading to schoolrooms, lights burning in houses where someone else's daughter, late at night, was reading and dreaming about her future?

***

The tragic events of October 9, 2012—another "shot heard 'round the world"—clearly were a clarion call to generations of women, and men, who recognized that the concept of education and living out one's dream is incredibly fragile. When Taliban assassins in the Swat Valley of Pakistan entered a school bus and targeted, and then shot, a young activist for women's education, each bullet was a message: Resistance to lives of power for women, even in this twenty-first century, is terrifyingly real.

The world watched and waited for news of that 15-year-old girl, Malala Yousafzai of Mingora in Pakistan's Khyber Pakhtunkhwa, who had been sentenced to death by extremists for writing a diary about life under the Taliban for BBC Urdu. We came to know her parents, Toorpekai and Ziauddin Yousafzai, who had so presciently named her after the Pashtun poetess and warrior, Malalai of Maiwand. They had held hopes for their only daughter's future. They too had wanted everything possible for her.

Through the months, we commiserated and prayed along with them for Malala's recovery in a British hospital. We heard the poignant words of her father: "When she fell, Pakistan stood." And it was with such gladness that her admirers learned of Malala's painstaking but hopeful recovery from her gunshot wounds.

Later, how extraordinary to see Malala walk through the halls of the United Nations, the scarf of Benazir Bhutto, assassinated leader of Pakistan, worn about her shoulders. To hear her wise words: "I raise up my voice—not so that I can shout, but so that those without a voice can be heard." In recognizing Malala's humility, courage, and wisdom, who could not be inspired by such a young woman?

Thus, I was honored to be asked to co-edit, with Joseph Hutchison, this anthology of poems dedicated to the work of Malala Yousafzai, who continues to be brave and smart and stubborn in her belief that, with education, the world is limitless for women.

***

Throughout the months after FutureCycle Press placed its Call for Submissions, poems flooded in daily. At first, they were poems of outrage, then sadness, then hope, then finally joy—poems from across this continent and around the world. Motifs evolved as Joe and I read hundreds of responses: land, sky, flight, flowers, daughters, dreams, mothers, rituals. While we ultimately selected poems with an emphasis on the central themes of the life and aspirations of Malala, we chose not to print poems that contained rants or invective. We admired poems that were heartfelt while demonstrating form or craft; poems with fresh viewpoints; poems that spoke to us—and even sang to us. The anthology came together while Malala healed, while the words we read helped us to heal too.

***

Today, as we appreciate the poems within, let this book be a global appeal for all children to expect the right to an education and to freedom of thought. One voice speaking out for so many others is really one hundred thousand voices—those pens and books and papers and poems—ennobling us all.

Malala, hold your head up high. Walk into the future.

—Andrea L. Watson

"One child, one teacher, one book and one pen
can change the world."

—MALALA YOUSAFZAI
"Malala Day" speech to the United Nations
July 12, 2013

Conrad DiDiodato

Malala

Malala—
  walking arm in arm,
    deep stairway

Joseph Hutchison

Malala

Malala—

the way forward's
always first

into darkness,
then through it—

the light you carry,
that old-soul courage—

millions will follow

Kathleen Dale

Wild Rhubarb

In a Pakistani school bus
one just her age is gunned down.

It is in a country where perfect
daughters of stunned women are married

at eight, or disfigured by bullets or acid,
their fierce zeal to learn, to choose, withered.

In *her* country, there are those who seek,
from behind the Cross, to direct

her body, husband the books *she* reads.
The summer she begins to bleed,

her parents' back lawn stretches flawless
save for one large weed in the epicenter.

Sent out to clear it, she kneels, pulls
off the toughest leaves, dark with toxin,

spies the wrist-thick, yellow rhizome
plugged deep into red, hard

Kansas clay. She begins to dig,
and as she sweats, learns something about

determination, about the wild, unruly
beauty of blemish; that despite the most

ferocious gods, new growth will push
forth lush, thicker, greener shoots.

Sherry Stuart-Berman

To the Taliban
Re: Malala Yousafzai, October 2012

You board the school bus, ask
for her by name: "She who has flow."

Grazed by the gun she
becomes that bird, that bird
on the back of your doubt
poised to remake your ruin
expose your rotting moment
to air.

What does it do to you—
your slack-eye, your skill—
when she rejects your dirt
as fallow, spits it out as rust?

The world will gape
pretend what happened
is new, assume your aim
was accidental.
She holds to her grit.
In the hospital room, in Swat Valley
grief sleeps.

Scientists say the molecules
in her mind are descendants

of shattered stars: She will
not be denied deep space
to inhabit, a reach to sketch
her milky way.

This one you must leave.
It is our honey.
It is our shot.

Pat Hanahoe-Dosch

Malala's Mother, the First Week

In what empty ravine of rocks and dirt
does her hungry mind drift now that we
can feed only her body, which we sting with fluids and medicine?
Once I starved to know more, too,
than how to cook dahl or pray for a calm house.
I could see the winds whirl the snows on the sharp, jagged
mountains that surround us and wanted to know
what stirred those icy flakes and currents
yet kept them there on those steep peaks
they cannot escape unless the wind blows them far enough down
to where they can melt in the sun, come summer and release.
I wanted to know how to read the Koran myself and not
depend on these sharp, jagged men
to tell me what it says I should be. I want
so much more for my daughter than I could ever swirl into
in this life. "Here is how you find
the area of a triangle," my husband, a teacher, once explained.
To know the depth of these mountains, to be able to calculate
the distance between them—that is the greatest gift
any of us can give her. She can read
the Koran. She knows
it does not forbid her an education.
These men are angry and afraid because they cannot tell her
what they want her to believe. She can
calculate the area between their sharp corners and betrayals.
She can be so much more than these mountains
have let me be. If only
she can heal enough now. If only

they have not caused such an avalanche
in her brain that she cannot climb back to me.
I listen to the sound of her labored breathing and I know
she is scaling the ridges and crevasses they have made.
I know she is gripping the rocks and ledges of her memory
and climbing slowly back to me, one handhold and foothold at a time.

Pat Hanahoe-Dosch

Malala

What is a symbol or a hero, but a human
story told over and over,
a photo, a name, a recounting,
a bullet in the head, blood smeared
across the wooden seats of a van?
She gives her story to us
for the others, left behind
among the veiled and scarved lives
in a space walled in
by some of the most beautiful mountains in the world.
Their treacherous, jagged peaks sharpen against the sky
while the snows swirl and avalanche across their faces,
scoring crevasses and dark scars across the rock
of their bodies like acid
thrown across the skin of girls
who want to learn enough to glimpse what might lie
beyond those impassable borders.
Mud brick and stone walls,
a few rugs, blankets and bitter winds
separate their villages from ours,
a deeper and colder rift than the expanse
between our continents.

Joan Colby

Choosing

At the canyon's rim,
a banquet of brush, scarlet hats
of maple, gold crowns of ash, rock
outcroppings. a signet gingko tree designed
for thoughts of paradise, or reading
a poem by Emily who hid her
words with silken ribbons.

Don't hide, don't listen to men who discourage
dreams or diminish with
consolation. Find the room
that Virginia spoke
of. Let the sunlight flood you with ambition.

In Pakistan, Malala Yousafzai,
aged 11, acknowledged such voices,
small fledglings that hatched
despite the Taliban, their beards
heavy with ownership:
A woman is property, an emblem
to masculine honor in her
silent obedience.

Malala chose and stepped
into the geography of knowledge.

Ed Baker

A Young Girl

a young girl goes
into a large
arena—

        it is not in
        the Land of Oz

not a fiction on a youngster's reading
list

        nor into a fiction of
        lions and tigers and bears

        no easy way to gain the freedom

to explore—

           a young woman bravely goes

Judith Terzi

Ode

She is a pool of gleam.
She is a seed, the rain.
She is a prairie of idea,
the harvest of motion.
She is rosewater
in a sandstone bowl.
She is the refugee, the tarp
of tent, the flame of fugue.
She is the arms of mothers,
a ribbon in a porcelain moon.
She is a lioness and loneliness,
the newborn swathed in blush.
She is earth yellow, jade,
aquamarine. She is the sea—
el mar, la mer, il mare, samandar.
She is a threshold, an arch,
a minaret. She is every headscarf—
magenta, celeste, amethyst.
She is majestic, *magnifique.*
She is a luminous lagoon.
She is our hands, our pen.
Malala.

Basia Miller

Prism of Light

Wherever it's found
light throws open windows,
unlatches gates,
loosens links that bind our bodies
and tie us to the ground.

Light breaks through silence, Malala,
as you speak to the leaders
of readings for girls,
of lessons shining.

Light converted the crack
of black bullets, Malala,
fired point-blank at your temple
where you rode unarmed
in a school bus in Swat:

bright images of you
bandaged in Birmingham
flashed on screens and
burst on the world like a prism.

The sight of your courage
inspires us, Malala.
We stand tall
because of many like you,
light-bearing girl.

Peg Quinn

Note to the Taliban

I heard how you boarded a van,
asked which girl was Malala,
then shot her in the head.

All that day I gathered my classes outside
to look at the sky, wanting to make sure
the children noticed enormous dark clouds
stealing our view of the mountains while
the sun's piercing light dazzled
the mounting storm's edges, creating
exquisite lines.

We had to shield our eyes.

Paul Hostovsky

This and Only This

Teach the women this and only this.
We have killed each other over the women.
We have killed ourselves over the women.
We have killed the women because the women
are so beautiful we want to die.

We must save the women from themselves.
We must save ourselves from the women.
Teach the women this and only this. They are
so beautiful we want to die. We must save them
for ourselves only, ourselves only, ourselves only.

Madelyn Garner

21 Grams

The virginal bride, who will spend
a lifetime wearing
the bullet wound as wedding ornament;

42 grams of her shadow sisters,
their schoolbooks
reddened by blood and sand.

The gunman believes
he's restored the landscape. Hoisted
onto the shoulders of men, he

is measured by grams of stacked bullets,
the bombs he will plant.
Meanwhile, his waiting family

is interrogated by shame. His sister weeps
apology on every channel.
The ululations of mothers join

all of those who have held the faceless,
the shackled, the bled
because of the word.

Silence—how many grams?

Aftab Yusuf Shaikh

Grief

Grief is the marble
with which all palaces
of hearts are built.

Grief is that agony
that wrecked the heart of Abraham
when he placed the dagger
on the neck of his lifelong prayer
in service to the Lord of all worlds.

Grief is that smile
on a mother's face after
she releases her child, when she bears
the bitterest pain of her life.

Grief is the warm tear
rolling down her cheek
when that same child
robs her of her rights.

What is grief?

Grief is
the bravest daughter of the soil
asking permission to breathe.

Linda Hogan

The Daughter of Eve

I grew up on knowledge.
I wore clothing
that covered everything.
I ate an apple a day
medicine
biting through the skin
because we couldn't afford
doctors.
That's why my brother died
while someone else became rich
and my father lost not only his rib
but his kidney to those who don't see us
and the bank called the world
fell and all I want to know
is what they call sin?

Me, I have never sinned
unless you call it
being alive.

Bobbi Lurie

Kabul

This afternoon I went to the jar, sank my finger in the honey.
No one saw me so I let the sweetness linger on my tongue.

At night I paint black around my eyes.
I wash it off at morning.

When everyone's asleep, I draw on scraps of paper
I've collected, the backs of labels, edges torn from newspapers.
This is my secret.

***

Coming back from the highway with my brothers,
I dropped my spade, went to lean against the shed,
Heard Father's voice coming from within.
He was laughing with Abdullah who says he'll buy me
For three bags of wheat
When Father's done with me.
When he does I'll slash my body with petrol,
Strike the match like Laida did.

I watched those two fools empty a giant vat of honey
Into another vat, saw them pull out long tubes
They scraped with their hands, licked with their tongues.
Beneath the amber honey, I saw guns.

Father caught me looking, jumped off his chair,
His hands were claws clipping toward me,
Shoving me hard against the wall, grabbing me *there*.

Whore! he screamed then spit on me.
I couldn't move. I couldn't speak.
I covered my face.

Back in the tent
Mother was making lentils,
Hunched over the fire.
I pulled the spoon from her hand, stirred the pot
As if I were her daughter.

***

Today, walking with my brothers, I saw Bashir.
He was leaning against a wall, one leg missing.
I knew, still a shock went through me
Seeing the dirty rags tied around his stump, the blood dried,
What looked like pus.
And how he stood as if he had a leg.
Strange how we never speak
But I walk through him with my eyes,
Enter his hidden rooms.
He was speaking with Khangal about the enemy
But his soft eyes were blazing holes in me,
Forcing me to see the sky and trees with deeper color.
Khangal saw me looking, threw his spade hard against my leg.
The pain was so intense. I bled and bled,
Putting pressure on the wound with just my hand.
My burqa drenched in blood,
He pulled me up by my hair.

I burned in the part of me which was not hurt.

***

Tonight Father had guests. I heard them say
They liked the bread.
I baked it
While Mother took a nap.
She did not say
I baked it. She turned her back to me.

***

I feel sickness inside me all the time.
I enter the back rooms with my father,
Creep out like a rat trapped in its maze,
Seek escape in the next cage where Mother stands
Brewing the food, keeping us snared in this affliction called life.
And I think of our martyrs dying for freedom.
I would like to die for freedom.
But I am a woman
And I do not believe in the paradise Father speaks about
While he beats me with his stick.

***

But every day I keep collecting my scraps of paper.
And when everyone's asleep,
I draw Bashir, his stump, my father with his guns,
My mother hunched over the fire stirring lentils.
I draw them all out of me.
I open myself to the darkness.
I wait for night to speak.

Kathleen Cain

Lingering

After the reading four women linger
over words. One recites a new work
from a poetry exercise: *to speak in the voice
of something else.* She lifts a box lid marked
in red, all caps: PARTS

and removes from tissue paper, as if it were
the Shroud of Turin, or the shin bone of some
virgin martyred saint, nearly three feet of tawny
hair, cut off when she was sixteen. *Deliberately*

is all she will say, without further explanation for
the shearing. She begins to apologize and give
away the poem. We shush her and implore: *Just read.*

Unbound from its cardboard coffin, the fall
shimmers under the stage light, still caught at
one end in a blue rubber band. Her words release it:

sun-catcher
flecked red and gold
set loose after scrubbing
to shine and flow over
her young self, still able
to speak, from every strand,
the distance of her life.

Karla Linn Merrifield

Homage to the Salix Women

I salute the willows of Mingora
along the river's southern margin,
always among the last trees
to loose their leaves.
I bow to their suppleness,
their sweeping majesty of green umbrellas
yellowing in morning sun-fog.
Mine is an obeisance
to their weeping grace in late season.
How like us they are
or we like them: bending
into tomorrow, our winter's rest.

Kathryn Winograd

etymology of girl

> The g-r words denote young animals, children, and
> all kinds of creatures considered immature, worthless,
> or past their prime

i won't say winter, or how the serial moon
bends the trees back thick in their dying

too much, we say, too much, this small girl, *what
is the grass,* a child once asked, and now this other girl,

heaps of grass tending (*how many*) the tender
body, the stolen, the would be stolen, here in this field, the girl's

arm tender, here the small shell of her ear
tender—such intimate scatter beneath this pulpit sky

cirro, nimbo, cumulo—i want the language of clouds, not
this language of daughters, of girls: curl of their hair,

their griefs, we want to think, still light as rain
how can we say the lyrical, say *deer, heart-track, gold stem,*

winter lonely, alone *blue moon* we say *blue moon*
something like gauze or veil held against the rookery

of mouth and its tiny birdsong
here are the roots of words i can give you:

malala: all-honey or *grief-stricken,* and you, dear dead girl
of the grass, *fetching it to me with full hands, God beholds*

blossoms, pearls, inner sea fold of petal, flower flesh—
what else did men name you centuries centuries

Ana Istarú

my mother's death has a name

[From *Verbo madre*, translated by Mark Smith-Soto]

my mother's death has a name
many names with first names and surnames

I know no one sweating bent over with pain
will go from door to door calling out
where is the schoolgirl
the one they bludgeoned to death
the town's powerful men
the ones who wrote around her neck
a stuttering red

I know no one paid for her ransom
Matilde dies

they throw her from the tile roof of the church
and then take communion from her skull

young she was a youthful girl
later my mother
later she wanted to touch the pieces of the game
throw the chess set over
enter like a woman in the circle of men
twisting as best she could the sharp edges
the dragon's teeth
trying to touch that pot of power
burning her hands with dignity
to twist
the pieces of that game
brandishing her truth

the dead schoolgirl was convinced
she was a queen trying to fly
she was in love
with this little plot of homeland
although that love sounded unpleasing
to the town's powerful men

.it doesn't matter
since she had much love of the good kind
and the concierges loved her
the common people and
the few honest men that still remain
the women loved her of course

she was a queen trying to fly
clutched to her decency to her armor
of incorruptible love

now she is dead
they killed her with cancer with weariness
with the gross gangrene of rage

they sealed her eyes they sold her
set fire to her senator's seat
to watch her in flames
to burn her
unmoved schoolgirl
incidentally they burned my mother

now they wear her ashes in their buttonholes

my mother's death has a name
many names with first names and surnames

right now they are resting in their houses
visiting their wounded mistresses

carrying their souls in a rotten glass
in truth
they act like they don't know

no difference

I have a corpse of gold
I have an inviolate death
I will go dancing down the street with her body
falling to crumbs
I have Matilde enough to tint the sea

them
when they see what they may see
let them see me

to burn a woman like Iphigenia

death will come to them soon enough
the terrible cramp
I will dance with them that day
and in that thick spider
of their heart
I will lay a burning blade my orphanhood

I will look at them
I will look at them

I will look at them

until then
them
when they see what they may see
let them see me
in the eyes of their children and their children
amen

Ana Istarú

A Daughter Leads Her Mother Into Sleep

[From *Verbo madre,* translated by Mark Smith-Soto]

I spoke with the piece of my mother
that didn't want to die   that wouldn't give...
that was the colt gone wild
and the live nerve severed in the face of death

so fierce the flaming from the sword she wielded
we had to bury her with her hands tied

I managed to speak with that cold jar
of blood that was about to die
I saw a god in pieces I saw a spike
of gunpowder in her breast

and to that small piece of her inner ear
that fluttered like a sacred silk
like the last sail
the final pulse of a flaming splinter

and to that fragment of mother yet remaining
that weighs more than the world
and is the boiling diamond
I bury between my eyes

to that jar of faith handed to me
by the sad merciful surgeons
I was able to speak
to say

good-bye little one
sleep
there will be no monsters in the dark

Ruth Obee

The Return of the Exiles

Under the black-turbaned militants
even the migratory birds were unable to sleep at night,
disturbed by the ceaseless fire of arms.

Ghazals were forbidden,
and Kabal's blind poet was no longer heard
to recite his poetry of unrequited love and longing.

The *rabaab* sat in its corner, strings without a melody—
silent as the bat-winged, anonymous women's
noiseless footfalls, the dawn-shrouded poor and maimed,
picking their way through the dust and rubble
of ruined streets.

It was a crime for them to be heard.

Nothing grew. Not vineyards or wheat, nor pomegranates.
Nothing grew under the sun
in this land of sand and snows, of high Himalayan peaks,
but death, dust, and destruction—the blood-red poppies
in the fields and the local warlord's beard.

But now again, after seven long years, *ghazals*
are being sung by singers and musicians—
songs to lure back the birds—
exiles returning from the ashes.

Marjorie Saiser

Margit, Age 24

Treblinka, Near Warsaw, 1942

Margit stands, naked, with others,
on the lip of the ditch,

the ditch dug for her,
for them.

If she looked up, she could see a row of soldiers,
a row of rifles, ready.

She looks down at the cold freckled skin of her arms;
she has crossed them in front of her.

Across the ditch:
a soldier in a line of soldiers.

My children, what have we taught you?
His shape, his shoulder, his rifle.

Her toes
in the fresh dirt.

Marjorie Saiser

I Have Nothing to Say About Fire

I have nothing to say about fire
except my father could build one
I saw his hands as he moved logs into place
his hands which I would know

anywhere I have nothing to say about hands
except his were old and
good I have nothing to say about good
except that it is connected with lucky

they are right and left hands: good and lucky
but good does not always mean lucky I could say something
about guilt because my sister on some other side of the world
to the left or right of lucky

is biting her lip tasting blood she may be
lying on a blanket thinking of pain
I have nothing to say because I have said it
and am lucky undeserving I

who did not earn did not choose did not merit.
I have nothing to say and I have time to say it
and people to listen. I have everything.

Sarah White

Of Emilie, Who Would Have Known...

Newtown, Connecticut, December 2012

It's what they knew that makes you wail:
how to tie a shoe, zip a coat,
do an alphabet with magic
markers and let it rhyme.

A student of mine learned by heart
a poem in a language not her own.
When she was lost I wailed: "Not Marian!
Not Marian!" Where is the poem

now that she is gone? Where's
the phrase to say *Good Morning,
Dad* in Portuguese? I am afraid

nobody says it any more, not even in Brazil,
since we lost Emilie, the only one
who would have known how to console us.

Jane Hirshfield

Like the Small Hole by the Path-Side Something Lives In

Like the small hole by the path-side something lives in,
in me are lives I do not know the names of,

nor the fates of,
nor the hungers of or what they eat.

They eat of me.
Of small and blemished apples in low fields of me
whose rocky streams and droughts I do not drink.

And in my streets—the narrow ones,
unlabelled on the self-map—
they follow stairs down music ears can't follow,

and in my tongue borrowed by darkness,
in hours uncounted by the self-clock,
they speak in restless syllables of other losses, other loves.

There too have been the hard extinctions,
missing birds once feasted on and feasting.

There too must be machines
like loud ideas with tungsten bits that grind the day.

A few escape. A mercy.

They leave behind
small holes that something unweighed by the self-scale lives in.

John Sibley Williams

Four Casings in an Endless Field

A single flash,
forgotten the moment it passes,
is enough
to divide the sky
forever.

***

The most glorious songs
passed down these long generations
and endlessly repeated over our cradles
like mantras
began as a terrible dissonance
tempered by hope.

***

Retreating to a peaceful time
that never existed
is still the dream
of every unspent cartridge.

***

Permanence means one thing
to the hand that fires,
something else entirely
to the voice that endures.

Desmond Kon Zhicheng-Mingdé

Grenouille Bleue

Maybe between shouts
an urging, stress of weather
like a fissure, an impasse.
Maybe a blanket?

A coat and towel too.
For the draftsman howling
at the sky, and angels
through the sugar maple.

Wading monastics
washing muslin robes.
Stalk of lemongrass in hand;
raw hemp around ankles.

Twelve shoes tethered,
laced into a bouquet—
quiet love seating itself.
Of moonstone and a dirt road.

Have the bluebells
turned cerulean? At sundown,
an emphatic stress. Of hope,
our soft bundle of ballads.

John Brandi

Rawali Siding

That it could be like this:
the old whitewashed station
shadowed with leaves, a gleaming bell
announcing the incoming Express,
three veiled women arm in arm
taking their time crossing the platform.

A man in knit cap,
sandals off, hands on knees,
rising from a prayer mat, handing
out sweets from a handspun tunic
to a circle of children.

Among passengers gathered
In freshly painted waiting rooms
no one afraid of the purse on the bench
or the box left alone on the counter.
No one strapped with anything
but suspenders.

John Brandi

Cutting Through the Morass

East of the Karakorams
ambling starry crags, I chisel a trail
above the world's haze.

No matter how far out I go
the news is always close. Monk, shepherd,
a baker in his shack tell stories
of another blown-up school,
teachers threatened, girls thrashed
by men who raise themselves high
              with eager stones.

I fix my walking stick into ice,
let breath dissolve into planet light.
I wonder how many families are sleepless
        tonight, on edge with fear?

By sunrise, I might cross the pass,
meet a soul-bright bloom on her way to school,
scout a new frontier, find an authentic man,
share tea, cup my hands
        around the gift of peace.

Ilmana Fasih

Malala

October 12, 2012

Urdu:

Andhon ko unka chehra dikha diya hai Malala ney.
Jehad dar-asl kya hai, sikha diya hai Malala ney.
Jahalat sey hai jang, jata diya hai Malala ney.
Taleem hai farz-e-momin, bata diya hai Malala ney.
Soye huwe seenon ko jaga diya hai Malala ney.
Khoye huwe iman se, mila diya hai Malala ney.
Payam-e-Amn duniya ko, suna diya hai Malala ney.
Her shakhs ko Malala, bana diya hai Malala ney.

English Translation:

The blind have been shown their real face by Malala.
What is true struggle has been taught to us by Malala.
The real fight is against ignorance, has been asserted by Malala.
Education is an obligatory duty of believers, as reminded by Malala.
Apathetic hearts have been shaken awake by Malala.
The lost message of faith has been rediscovered by Malala.
The message of Peace to the World has been conveyed by Malala.
Each one of us feels Malala, has been made possible by Malala.

Ken Meisel

Malala (Grief-Stricken)

"*Grief-stricken* is a name I'd use for it,"
the cleric said to his student

as they strolled through the rose garden
to examine the stomped roses.

Above them, the empty blue sky;
around them, noisy school buses.

"Someone must have come here
under cover of cloak or domain,

perhaps enraged at the sight of roses
where before there was just rubble,

or perhaps it was just the old gardener
who could not tolerate—" that was

the word he used in conversation
with his student—"could not tolerate

the way the earth must always renew
itself in beauty," and kneeling down

the cleric held the rose head in his
hand to highlight the red twirls of it

to his student who kneeled there
beside him, eyes bright and curious,

and he called it *feminine,* by the pronoun,
Malala—"this condition of the world

we find ourselves involved in,
this one enduring rose that survived."

Penn Kemp

Malala

October 13, 2012

Malala, your name sounds like a song
but it means grief-stricken in Urdu,
language of poets. You are named
after a poet, a warrior woman, and
you have so lived up to your name.

The courage it takes to cross borders
defined by others, courage to uphold
freedom to read, learn, speak—to be
fully the human that is all our birthright.

"Every girl in Swat is Malala. We will
educate ourselves. We will win. They
can't defeat us," states her classmate.

Now it's our turn to take up the call,
education for every child for which
women and girls today rally across
India, Pakistan and Afghanistan lands.

Malala, Malala. I hear the ululation
of lament and of celebration for her.
Can you hear what she's crying? You
can join her common cause. But how
fares the girl in her hospital bed now?

That beautiful face blasted. Her voice
silenced, her eyes shut. Hang on, girl,
hang on. There's work to be done and we
desperately need such spirit among us.

Grief is no time for emotion. Let sky open
and open to more sky. Light, we call for
light to dispel the darkest oppression. Her
name on a million lips in many tongues.
Malala, Malala, Malala. Hear the ululation
and respond.

Barbara Rockman

Letter of Intent to Adopt

Santa Fe, New Mexico, USA to
Mingora, Swat Valley, Pakistan

Schools shut their doors in protest and Pakistanis
across the country held vigils to pray for a 14-year old
girl who was shot by a Taliban gunman after daring to
advocate for girls' education.
—October 2012

Malala, there is music in your name
and something bitter between your teeth
that, swallowed, turns sweet:

I who have grown daughters
have made a bed for you
in North America where

the aspens declare radiance;
the sumac, ovation of lit matches
raised to the singer. You are brave

beyond these trees that shed light
and leave us lonely. When I say *Malala*
walking my daily walk,

when I pray your name
in the night, there is spinning, glide
and a partner's low dip. You

will hum in my hallway as you
drop parcels and garments
before you slam out to the new world.

I am left with the clearing of my throat,
with my daughters' abandoned poems.
Even as we have been schooled

in a country of schools, still
we are women, Malala.
How badly we need the protest

you practice and insist the world repeat.
Season of lament and the trees! The trees as they float
letters to what cannot last. But still, still Malala,

the bright syllables of your name.

Diana Woodcock

Vani Brides of Pakistan

inspired by a BBC report, December 6, 2005

In the photograph we sit
side by side, only hands and eyes
uncovered—enough to tell
we're young and lovely—three
sisters fallen victim to Vani:

promised to the enemy; blood feud
settled by forced marriage, we brides
to spend our days as slaves paying
for a male relative's crime.
Illegal, it happens all the time.

But we three will resist though
the other side insists their honor's
been insulted: sisters must be handed
over, or fighting will result in
two hundred-plus deaths.

Father's on our side,
insisting we hide and continue
our studies. *My daughters
are innocent,* he insists, refusing
to let them squelch our dreams.

If unsuccessful in resisting,
we'll burn ourselves alive.
Law, religion, family's on our side.

Michael G. Smith

Poem for Three Women of the World

i. Mussoorie, India

Child, shoeless and filthy, walking this winter
street with intention, I say the tree buds and buds.

ii. Kathmandu, Nepal

Toddler holding my hand, abandoned, fatherless
by law and not a citizen, I say you are a blossom.

iii. Mingora, Pakistan

Young woman, to you I would say your life is a divine
sword, your calculus, the victor's gold leaf.

Michael G. Smith

Because of That, There Is This

Because of curious children,
    bees dance on the stage.

Because of starry heights,
    footsteps pepper wild trails.

Because of October's harm,
    November's refuge asks

an ancient faith to abide
    women creating honey,

their scholarship spreading
    wisdom over the sands.

Rita Brady Kiefer

Meteors

Did your eyes flash terror when they hijacked your school bus,
one of the men snarling your name down the aisle,
scanning each innocent face before lighting on yours?
What images blazed just before the bullet
grazed your luminous brain, sweet Malala?
At the hospital did you have nightmares: Taliban
instead of your loved olive trees in the orchards
outside your father's classroom, a thousand
points of grief webbing your mother's face?
Or did you dream bright streaks shooting across
a black sky? Not disembodied particles of dust
but flesh-and-blood women, subversive sisters
from the past? Were their stories familiar?

    A 17th century girl so bent on learning
    she hid her body under boys' clothes to go to school.
        A Mexican nun, reproached in an open letter
        by a bishop masked with a woman's name
        replied with a learned defense of girls'
        and women's *right* to study.
    A female German mystic eleven centuries back
    who depicted God as female.

Why do we doubt the sky is filled with history?

At eleven, Malala, you blogged:
Why aren't girls allowed to learn?
I want to read books. I want to write them.

Incandescent little rebel, you've already begun.

Rita Brady Kiefer

Letter: Little Daughter

Dear Phuonglinh—

Remember that June rain slanting the world
outside *A Woman's Place,* the shelter
where we met that night. Inside,
you, fifteen, learning to negotiate two languages,
mine and your mother's. Before the TV she sits
devouring images that litter an American screen
spitting alien sounds while you and I try to make
sense of some words we're committing
to paper: your story of crossing the country to escape
a father's fists, my trying to breathe in all I'm learning here.

I ask you to write the meaning of your name
in a poem you say you *can't make,* but I tell you
       you can.
So you begin: *my name means phoenix, a bird
that rises from its ashes.* Later when you read
aloud, you pause long before the line
every one hundred years it burns.

Now twenty years later I wonder where
this phoenix has flown. New York? San Francisco?
Her mother's Vietnam village?

Phuonglinh, wherever you are,
know there are poems the world needs
to read, if only you'll write them.

Lyn Lifshin

Malala Dreams of Helicopters

no longer throwing
toffee from the sky
but filling the air
with darkness. She
could hear artillery
fire. By morning
half the girls kept
coming to school.
On her way home
she heard a man say
"I will kill you."
It sounded like a
requiem. Withered
leaves fell through
her hair as if she
was still dreaming.
Dark birds of her
dreams plunging
in flame onto hill
sides that once
looked as if they'd
been dipped in beauty.

Lyn Lifshin

On the Day Rushing to the Metro
Already a Little Late on My Way to Ballet
I Nearly Skid on Acorns, Catch Myself

I think of Malala, maybe rushing, never
wanting to think her name means "grief
stricken." Maybe she was humming
a song she heard once on TV
before the Taliban banned it or
was watching leaves drift from the bus
or giggling with girl friends. Maybe
she was thinking of being a doctor and
coming back to treat young children
in her region, her Swat. Or maybe she
was hoping to see a certain boy with
licorice eyes and a smile who always
made her giggle. No longer able to wear
school uniforms, told to wear plain
clothes, Malala wrote in her blog,
Instead, I decided to wear my favorite
pink dress. Maybe the last beautiful
thing she saw as the bullet entered her
mahogany curls until later she woke
up in the hospital's cone of light.

Joan Roberta Ryan

The Pink Dress

I take my granddaughter to Nordstrom's.
She picks out a pile of lively pink dresses,
berry-pinks, fuchsia, salmon, flamingo,
tries the hot raspberry with sequin hearts,
spins out to the mirror, auburn braids dancing.
I hear a pale murmur of *redheads in pink,*
look at the price tag and catch my breath.

My mind springs from
my Lila to Malala, blossoming
at school in her berry-bright dress,
barred from classes and bold, active color
by men who cage daughters in draperies of black,
and I pray her clear voice and spirit prevail.

At the register, I buy the pink dress.

Diana Anhalt

Priorities

> How dare the Taliban take away my basic right to
> education?
>   —Malala Yousafzai, September 2008

When I was eleven, all I wanted
was an Everybody's Sweetheart Dress
with matching slippers to turn me
from dirty-necked kid with dandruff,
scabbed knees and hand-me-downs
into a princess.

But Malala yearns to clothe herself
in learning, would give her life to open
the doors of that closet-sized world
which strives to button her down,
to shroud her in darkness.

Me? I would have given my life
for a dress like Shirley Temple's—
sunset-blushed satin, ribbons
and lace—a dress the color of my face
when I think, now, of what Malala wants.

Carol Alena Aronoff

A Touch of Fashion

She wore a dress of feathers.
She was sister to the moon,
stoned for her healing touch.

She wore the robe of Isis,
priestess of the north wind,
beaten for her sacred touch.

She wore gold-threaded silk,
this Maharani daughter,
burned for her widow's touch.

She wore a silk cheongsam,
first child in a Chengdu family,
killed for her baby's touch.

She wore a dress of kente cloth,
servant to a queen, secret place
cut for her sensual touch.

She wore a woolen head scarf,
this brave Pakistani schoolgirl,
shot for learning truth's touch.

Carol Alena Aronoff

Letter to the Parents of
Prospective Suicide Bombers

Who will tend your olive groves when you are old,
rebuild your war-torn houses, find treasures
in the rubble of innocent lives?

I haven't walked in your shoes, buried good men,
felt your despair. My heart has not been torn by death—
of a child, a family, whole neighborhood.

I cannot tell you how to live,
whom to trust—or hate. But I can beg
for the lives of your children.

I weep for children everywhere: hungry,
afraid, alone. But especially for those we raise
to bomb themselves—and others.

There has to be another door that opens
into light, where everyone sits at the same
table, listening to children's laughter.

Jane Hilberry

In Arabic

On the phone, the teenage girl speaks a language
her stepsisters don't understand, a language
she makes into gravel to fling at her father

across a thousand miles. When she hears
his voice, like a mood ring set on a stove,
the atmosphere around her turns dark purple

spiked with yellow-green knives. He tells her
to cover her neck and head. She sounds
as if she were being strangled,

scraping the bottom of a river whose current
presses her under. Water can take a girl
and pin her to a rock, as an uncle pushes a child

against a wall, his hand bigger than her face.
In Amman, women stream the streets,
heads scarved. Some paint their hands

with intricate, hennaed patterns,
like the swirls this girl now doodles on her fist
in blue pen, a design with four quadrants,

a symmetry so confident it must have arisen
from beneath her skin. Will she survive?
She has her compass. She has her knives.

Kathleen Cerveny

At Fourteen

Who was I at fourteen? Who were you?
Diverted from the real by lives of ease,
could we have stood up, then, and claimed our due

as humans growing hungry for the new
excitement of the mind—things never seen?
Who was I at fourteen? Who were you?

A girl has stood against her world. She drew
the fire of those who guard what's always been
and stood steadfast against them, claimed her due.

Her courage is a brush that paints a view
of human worlds more worthy—rarely seen
by coddled ones, like me, like you.

The cowards' bullets aimed to silence truth;
pierce brain and tongue—still both thought and speech.
She fell, but has not failed to claim her due.

And has the fight for rights now been renewed
by blood, the hunger of one child to learn?
This girl of fourteen shames both me and you
if we don't stand—demand what we all are due.

Colleen Powderly

Nice Girls

Only nice girls need apply, no warriors or warhorses,
no advocates or champions of fairness or equity.

Only good girls who learn to creep through the night
or hide under blankets and stay out of sight.

Only paper girls who play lifelong their childhood dolls,
loose tabs neatly folded out of unsightly view.

Only sweet women wanted, not those who nurture strongly,
demand the price of honesty as they force it from themselves.

But warriors who dare speak for truth as they can see it,
who grow power in their hearts and wear it fearlessly,

can stand in the rooms of their grandmothers' glories,
tell their true stories out loud and free.

Kishwar Naheed

We Sinful Women

[From *Tablet & Pen: Literary Landscapes from the Modern Middle East,* translated by Rukhsana Ahmad]

It is we sinful women
who are not awed by the grandeur of those who wear gowns
who don't sell our lives
who don't bow our heads
who don't fold our hands together.

It is we sinful women
while those who sell the harvests of our bodies
become exalted
become distinguished
become the just princes of the material world.

It is we sinful women
who come out raising the banner of truth
up against the barricades of lies on the highways
who find stories of persecution piled on each threshold
who find the tongues that could speak have been severed.

It is we sinful women
now even if the night gives chase
these eyes shall not be put out.
For the wall that has been razed
don't insist now on raising it again.

It is we sinful women
who are not awed by the grandeur of those who wear gowns
who don't sell our lives
who don't bow our heads
who don't fold our hands together.

Abigail Wyatt

Holy Housework

> In response to Father Piero Corsi, who called on
> Italian women to engage in "healthy self-criticism"
> over the issue of men murdering women

Today we must shake out our spotted sheets
and bring our soiled linen to the light;
we must fall on our knees confessing our faults
and scour our kitchens for stains;
and with what stern purpose we must seek
those specks that infect our murky hearts,
sweep them out and sluice them down,
our starkest imperfections undone.
And, today, too, we must lather and scrub
till our sins are all rinsed clean;
when our souls will shine like brand-new pins
where seraphim may dance if they will;
and today we must launder the rags of our guilt
and lift and beat the carpets of our shame,
bleach the great bowl of our wanton lust
and not omit to scrub around the rim.
We must roll up our sleeves and find His grace
in the scalding and the starching of our hearts,
our salvation in our cooking pots,
our glory in the great gift of our days.
All this we must do with a blessing on our lips
and humility and patience in our hearts;
but, Father, take heed, we are half of all there is
and, in sisterhood, we sing and we shine.

Paula J. Lambert

Anatomy of Birds, Part 1: Furcula

The work of soaring is arduous,
requires more than muscle alone,
requires the delicate architecture
of mostly hollow bone. The fused
and forked clavicle of a bird—
we call it the wishbone—
allows her to bear the rigors of flight,
stretching and then recoiling
with each powerful wingbeat. (Can
you hear it? The fiercely whispered
whoosh slicing air?) Downstroke
and release. Let's call it resilience,
what pushes the songbird forward,
what propels the hawk! Oh, let's
remember this living bone can flex!

April Bulmer

Dove Tale

A mourning dove rests on her soft nest
in a window box among my pink petunias.
Her eggs fragile, but warm as stones.
I do not coax her with crumbs
or the memory of flight,
the quick river hatching fish below.
She is a devoted mother—
more than feathers, wings,
a soft sack of bones.
Crouched among the blooms,
I imagine she rehearses a silent poem;
it does not rhyme with "flowers."
Perhaps her mind is still as Buddha's,
does not rise and fall like mine,
hatch like the moon, wax or wane or sigh.

CB Follett

Horses of Pain

To ride on horses of pain and remembering,
where fires ignite the rivers
and soldiers with lamp-blacked boots
thunder on cobbles;
to ride to the place of no escape
where the green flash is as quick
as a shot to the head,
where crops lie flattened
and a woman keens by a broken wall,
where rib-latticed dogs scavenge
and a bucket of water is worth more than gold.

Along the street where markets stood
pools the rust of yesterday's blood.
To live like this or die without warning,
to wonder when your son will come home,
how your daughter can be kept hidden
as your house falls in; donkeys run toward the hills
and a youth with burning eyes wears
a girdle that will blow him into the stars;
where mouths pucker but no spit comes
and the peach tree withers
that once was the bounty of summer.

Vassilis Zambaras

Mirror Image

For those who see that *evil* looks
Like *live* written backwards
(And for those who cannot),

Let us live for that day when
We see evil come up from behind us
And no one looks away.

Vassilis Zambaras

World Geography Lesson

1.

    (1950)

Home was where

The few dying
Embers of the olive

Were always warm
Enough to warm

The cold, weathered insoles
Of our shoes

Before we trudged
Off to school.

2.

School was where
The teacher kept warm

By thrashing us
With an olive stick

When the answers
To his questions

Were not what he wanted
To hear.

3.

The first flowers caught
Rearing their heads

Through the snow
Were always wild

Yellow crocuses in early,
Early spring.

4.

    (2012)

Half-way across the world, home was where
Such a flower spoke

A language the Taliban did not want to hear.

Forugh Farrokhzad

I Will Greet the Sun Again

[From *Sin: Selected Poems of Forugh Farrokhzad,*
translated by Sholeh Wolpé]

I will greet the sun again,
greet the stream that once flowed in me,
the clouds that were my unfurling thoughts,
the aching growth of the grove's poplars
who passed with me through seasons of drought.
I will greet the flock of crows
who gifted me the grove's night perfume
and my mother who lived in the mirror
and was my old age's reflection.
Once more I will greet the earth
who, in her lust to re-create me, swells
her flaming belly with green seeds.

I will come. I will come. I will.
My hair trailing deep-soil scents.
My eyes intimating the dark's density.
I will come with a bouquet picked
from shrubs on the other side of the wall.
I will come. I will come. I will.
The doorway will glow with love
and I will once again greet those in love, greet
the girl still standing in the threshold's blaze.

Andrea L. Watson

All the Ways You Know to Love Us

ghazal for asa

We are blaze you find such dangerous beauty—
A thousand jewels confined as dangerous beauty.

Veil us in raven-cloth. Paint our windows jet.
For centuries defined: Danger is beauty.

Stone us, ask us to eat your fallen fruit:
Skin is opal rind of danger-etched beauty.

Beat us; brand us; bind our rubied feet.
Ancients declare our kind *danger* (if beauty).

O, cut out our tender lotus, moist pearl
On which you dined with danger as beauty.

Press us with rocks for two darkling moles;
Obsidian refined what danger owes beauty.

Carve our amber breasts. Adorn us in radium.
Silver strands entwined—Danger us, beauty.

Array us in shrouds of sapphired weave:
Widow-cloth designed for danger in beauty.

Burn us with eternity husbands, onyx
Ash refined to danger...risk...beauty.

Pretend the sky is blind to dangerous beauty—
Sun's topaz eye divined such dangerous beauty.

Wayne Lee

Song for Rahim Alhaj

Chords like cries from rubble
his head bent over his *oud*

he cradles her in his lap
her carved neck angled back

strums like breath
plays the light back into the moon

wind rustles dry leaves
tears fall like shooting stars

embers in the night
he carries his mother in his eyes

smoke masking clouds·
cousins assassinated at taxi stands

first song he ever heard
last song his mother sang

Iraqi lullaby

he cradles her in his lap

Meryl Stratford

How the Night Fish Live

after Adrienne Rich's *Diving into the Wreck*

First having learned the Koran by heart,
every word of its six hundred pages,
and in a foreign language,
I put on
my black abaya
that covers me from head to toe.
I am having to do this
not like my father or my
carefree brothers
who play on the sun-drenched beach
but like the woman
I should become.

There is the ocean.
The ocean is always there,
restlessly heaving.
The men know what it is for,
the men with their fishing nets.
For me
it's a great mystery.

I enter it
step by step until
the water welcomes me,
black water under black sky
lit only by stars.
I enter it

and there is no one
to tell me where this ocean
will take me.

First the water is warm and then
it is cool, then cooler and then
it is cold like those faraway oceans of ice.
My mind is a vessel
pumped full of all they have taught me.
It is a knife, a camera, a compass,
a powerful tool.
The ocean is another story,
a six-hundred-page poem
in a foreign language,
a world I explore
by myself.

And now: I will never forget
what I came for
here among the many who have always
lived here,
swimming with luminous bodies
through the pregnant dark.

I came to explore a wreck.
Words are purposes. My mother says
You must tell your father.
Words are maps. My father says
She will be a housewife.
I came to see the damage that was done—
erasing faces with acid,
setting wives on fire—
and the treasure that was lost.
I slip out of my black abaya
and swim naked in the sea.

The thing I came for:
truth, the mother tongue,
evidence of damage.
The ravaged face always hidden
behind curtain or wall,
the ribs of a starving child
clothed in threadbare beauty.

This is the place.
And I am here.
My sisters swim silently
around me.

We are the golden ones
born of yesterday's sunsets.
We are rays of light
searching night's ocean,
eyes open wide, wondering
how we came to this world.
We dart and shimmer. We
breathe black water.

Meryl Stratford

Her Education

Into the quiet classroom
of the mind comes flying
the furious teacher with a lesson
of fear. This *bullet*
is not a bullet, it's merely
a word, something the mouth
makes for the delicate ear,
something the breath sends
that troubles the air, a ballet
of sound moving through silence
that explodes in an image as sudden
as death. Where is the wound?
It bleeds in the minds of a million
grief-stricken girls. They will be
pilots, doctors, warriors,
poets. They will sit on the ground
in the dust, just to learn.
In the twenty-first century,
every girl is Malala.

Susan J. Erickson

Given Fire, Given Water

Italicized lines by Kishwar Naheed

Malala would not let stone men silence her voice.
We hear her call. Our answer? Mend the fabric
of goodwill with the warp and weft of free voices.

Note the female kingfisher's red-banded breast.
Why not display our wounds as marks of honor?
Blood may flow as we deliver our voices.

How small these grains of rice! Given fire, given
water, they swell and stick together—perfume
the air with an irrefutable voice.

*The idea of making a footpath was a good
one.* We will have to find a way when *sickness
stalks the world* to tend each true-throated voice.

Our task is to be as resourceful as cornflowers.
Haven't you seen how a whole field of blossoms
can crowd out the thistles of fearful voices?

Susan, you read books in a library,
carry its card with your name. Still you can
pledge "I am Malala" in an ink-black voice.

Anita Jepson-Gilbert

For Malala on Her 16th Birthday

Dear Malala,
In our country, yours and mine,
hundreds of schools have been bombed
and burned to the ground.
My own in Karachi no longer stands,
and girls are dying all over Pakistan
from their hunger to learn.
How those men hate our schools.

Now my father keeps me at home
to learn from my brothers and their books.
I'm learning new English words now
by finding the translation of the names
of so many who have died
for going to school here.

In Islamabad, there was Halima,
which translates as *gentle, patient,*
from Amal, I learned *hope,*
and from Ghada, *beauty.*
In Swabi, there was Ishraq, *radiance,*
and from Tahira I learned *purity.*

In Quetta, there was Nur,
which I learned is *light,*
and from Latifa, I learned *kindness,*
from Sabat, *truth,*
from Nunat, *blessings,*
and from Khalida, I learned *immortality.*

And for your birthday, dear Malala,
I gather each of these, like precious jewels,
chanting their names in Arabic and English,
and send them all to you. For their sake,
please don't stop speaking out
for me and all our sisters.

With love and respect,
I remain Khawlah,
which now I know
means *lonely.*

Katherine L. Gordon

Into the Light

Malala, Malala, your lullaby name
comforts earth's children
who cringe at the shame
of tearing out flowers, bloodying beauty,
ravaging courage with gunshots of pain.
Tyrants fear Truth that wears power down
like the wind and the rain on dark mountains,
patiently surviving grim ages
to shine in the faces of girls
who know what reverence will bring:
less anger, less war, more sharing, more plenty
the powerful gift of love—
education for mothers to lift up children,
help men through the burdens
of problems to come.
Malala is the beacon that shepherds
each struggling gender
into the light.

Sholeh Wolpé

The Rosetta Stone

Sakineh is a popular name.
Means quietude.
Also, feminine.

Saket 'o Samet is a compliment
paid to young women,
scoring them marriage points.
Meaning: silent and mute.

Saleeteh is an insult reserved only for women.
Means: one who bothers men; a shrew.

Bakereh is a girl with an "unstained skirt,"
a "Miss" as in a girl not yet married.
A female virgin.

And *Bakereh-shenasi* is a specialty.
Means parthenology, a word not found
in most English dictionaries.

Sholeh Wolpé

Pickles and Donuts

Cold basements remind me of the dead
fruit my mother smothered in sugar, the phallic
pickles souring in tight-lipped jars.

I keep my school uniform stained, my
long hair pulled back tight, my walnut
breasts cloaked with baggy shawls,

tell my friend next door, about the red
jam donut beneath our skirts, teach her
the waist-twisting dance of wrapping childhood's
curtain around her body so soon unfolded
like voodoo air from an uncapped perfume bottle.

I breathe in books that turn my eyelashes
to blue feathers, my eyelids' veins into delicate
wing-bones that flap and lift, travel me
to an island house on stilt legs.

She eats the stone pages of an old Quran,
comes of age at dusk where bombs fall
on paved roads and the sky rains scalding
lava that streams and streams, carries her
to the sharp edge of the world.

Chris Ransick

Ghazal for a Murdered Poet

for Nadia Anjuman, November 8, 2005

This morning when I heard, I looked in your eyes to find words,
hoping, though we speak different tongues, I might find words.

But those I found said only they discovered you too late,
bleeding on the floor, though they tried to find words.

Your husband said he beat you with his hands. He won't
allow an autopsy, afraid the doctors' hands might find words

to accuse him, written there in your blood, as a poem.
When his own last breath comes, may he sigh and find no words.

This evening, I watch rising hawks, turning under faint stars
in slow, distant circles and there, for you, I find words.

Ellen Bass

Bearing Witness

For Jacki Phoenix

> If you have lived it, then
> it seems I must hear it.
> —Holly Near

When the long-fingered leaves of the sycamore
flutter in the wind, spiky
seed balls swinging, and a child throws his aqua
lunch bag over the school yard railing, the last thing,
the very last thing you want to think about
is what happens to children when they're crushed
like grain in the worn mortar of the cruel.

We weep at tragedy, a baby sailing
through the windshield like a cabbage, a shoe.
The young remnants of war, arms sheared and eyeless,
they lie like eggs on the rescue center's bare floor.

But we draw a line at the sadistic,
as if our yellow plastic tape would keep harm
confined. We don't want to know
what generations of terror do to the young
who are fed like cloth
under the machine's relentless needle.

In the paper, we'll read about the ordinary neighbor
who chopped up boys; at the movies we pay
to shoot up that adrenaline rush—
and the spent aftermath, relief
like a long-awaited piss.

But face to face with the living prey,
we turn away, rev the motor, as though
we've seen a ghost—which, in a way, we have:
one who wanders the world,
tugging on sleeves, trying to find the road home.

And if we stop, all our fears
will come to pass. The knowledge of evil
will coat us like grease
from a long shift at the griddle. Our sweat
will smell like the sweat of the victims.

And this is why you do it—listen
at the outskirts of what our species
has accomplished, listen until the world is flat
again, and you are standing on its edge.
This is why you hold them in your arms, allowing
their snot to smear your skin, their sour
breath to mist your face. You listen
to slash the membrane that divides us, to plant
the hard shiny seed of yourself
in the common earth. You crank
open the rusty hinge of your heart
like an old beach umbrella. Because God
is not a flash of diamond light. God is
the kicked child, the child
who rocks alone in the basement,
the one fucked so many times
she does not know her name, her mind
burning like a star.

Diane Kistner

The Lamps of Night

Child, the lamps of night
burn brightly, softly, as you sleep,
though you in your bed of feathers
may not see them.

The night birds and the bats,
the soft grey feathered moths,
are diving through the streetlamps
as you sleep.

The stars are out now,
flying in circles,
and so are the fireflies,
flying in circles
of circles.

Glow worms lie
radiant under straw,
little curled fingers of light,
curled as the moon,
ringed in jewels,
secure in their beds
of straw and leaves
and feathers.

Out in the wood,
near a darkened pool,
stones that no one sees
are glowing,
golden.

There are others too,
enduring and subtle,
lamps of magic, elves' lamps,
lamps of dreams,
and the tiny lamps
the moon lights
on the leaves
of all the trees.

Contributors

RUKHSANA AHMAD has written and adapted several plays for the stage and radio. *The Hope Chest* was her first novel. A short story collection, *True Love and Other Stories,* is forthcoming. She is working on her second novel and adapting Nadeem Aslam's *Maps for Lost Lovers* for the screen. *We Sinful Women,* her pioneering translation of Urdu feminist poetry, is widely taught. She has also translated Altaf Fatima's novel, *The One Who Did Not Ask.*

DIANA ANHALT, a former resident of Mexico City, moved to Atlanta, Georgia, three years ago to be closer to family. She is the author of *A Gathering of Fugitives: American Political Expatriates in Mexico 1947-1965*; two chapbooks, *Shiny Object*s and *Second Skin*; and essays, articles, and book reviews in both English and Spanish. Most recently, her poems have appeared in *Nimrod, Atlanta Review, Comstock Review,* and *Passager.*

CAROL ALENA ARONOFF, a psychologist and writer, helped guide a Buddhist Meditation center, taught Eastern spirituality and healing practices at San Francisco State, and has led Healing in Nature retreats in Hawaii and Arizona. Author of *Compassionate Healing: Eastern Perspectives* and co-author of *Practical Buddhism: The Kagyu Path,* her collections of poetry and photographs are *The Nature of Music, Her Soup Made the Moon Weep, Cornsilk,* and *Blessings From an Unseen World.* Her poems have been published in *Comstock Review, Poetica, In Our Own Words, Mindprints,* and elsewhere, including several anthologies.

ED BAKER was born in Washington, D.C., in April 1941. He is now (in August 2013) living in Washington, D.C. Everything in between is in the art and in the poetry.

Poetry books by ELLEN BASS (ellenbass.com) include *Like a Beggar* and *The Human Line* (both from Copper Canyon) and *Mules of Love* (BOA Editions, Ltd.). She coedited *No More Masks!* (Doubleday), the first major anthology of poetry by women. Her work has been published in hundreds of journals and anthologies, including *The New Yorker, The Atlantic, The New Republic, Ploughshares, The American Poetry Review,* and *The Kenyon Review.* She currently teaches in the MFA program at Pacific University in Oregon.

JOHN BRANDI's publications include poetry, travel essays, modern American haiku, hand-colored broadsides, and limited-edition letterpress books. His work has been published in India, Nepal, and Europe. Among his books of poetry are *In What Disappears, Water Shining Beyond the Fields, Heartbeat Geography, Weeding the Cosmos* and *That Back Road In.* Prose includes *A Question of Journey* and *Reflections in the Lizard's Eye.*

APRIL BULMER is an award-winning Canadian poet living in Cambridge, Ontario. She holds three master's degrees in creative writing, religious studies, and theological studies. Known for her poetry of feminist spirituality, she has published seven books. Her newest volume of poetry is *Women of the Cloth* from Black Moss Press.

KATHLEEN CAIN, a poet and writer living in Arvada, Colorado, has close ties with her home state of Nebraska. She understands the agony of having a child savagely attacked: In 1993 her twenty-year-old stepson David was murdered in Aurora, Colorado. She will never understand what motivates people to harm children but never stops hoping that all people in the world will work to protect them and bring justice to those who harm them. Her poetry has recently appeared in *Collecting Life: Poets on Objects Known and Imagined* and is forthcoming in *The Untidy Season: An Anthology of Nebraska Women Poets.*

KATHLEEN CERVENY—artist, poet, and a Cleveland, Ohio, haiku champion—is currently Poet Laureate of Cleveland Heights. Since 1991, she has been the Director of Arts Initiatives for the Cleveland Foundation. As Cleveland Public Radio's producer and broadcast journalist for the arts (1987-90), she won 15 top awards and produced many features for National Public Radio. Her poems have appeared in Southern New Hampshire University's *Amoskeag,* the online journal *Shaking Like a Mountain,* in Pudding House Press journals, and elsewhere.

JOAN COLBY has published widely in journals such as *Poetry, Atlanta Review, South Dakota Review,* and more, and has received many awards for her work, including an Illinois Arts Council Fellowship. She has published eleven books, most recently *Joan Colby: Selected Poems* from FutureCycle Press. Colby is the editor of *Illinois Racing News* and lives on a small horse farm in northern Illinois.

KATHLEEN DALE (kathleenanndale.squarespace.com) is a semi-retired teacher with three grown daughters. As a sustaining member of Women for Women International, she has for many years supported education for women in all countries, including Afghanistan and Pakistan. Her most recent chapbooks include *Rescue Mission* (Antrim House Press) and *Ties that Bind* (Finishing Line Press). Her work appears online in *The Centrifugal Eye*. *Avatars of Baubo,* a chapbook, is forthcoming.

CONRAD DIDIODATO is a poet, blogger, and secondary school teacher with work published in *World Haiku Review, LYNX: A Journal for Linking Poets, Tower Poetry, Voices Israel, Poemata, Ascent Aspirations* and *The Offending Adam.* His first book of poetry, *Bridget Bird and Other Poems,* was released in 2012. He wrote the Foreword to Ed Baker's *Stone Girl E-Pic* (2011) and is presently writing a literary biography of American poet Frank Samperi.

LAURA EKLUND (lauraeklund.org) is known in the United States and abroad for her non-objective and abstract paintings. Both her painting and writing are an extension of her own mythography—a private world of metaphor, color, dreams, symbols, and words. Also a published poet, Eklund sometimes incorporates collage, writing, and mixed media in her paintings. She represented the U.S. in the Florence Biennale in 2009 and has since secured an international presence, exhibiting in four different countries.

SUSAN J. ERICKSON lives in Bellingham, Washington, where she helped establish the Sue C. Boynton Poetry Walk. She is currently working on a manuscript of poems in women's voices, so she was inspired to write a ghazal on the impact of Malala's voice. Samples of her poems appear online at 2River.org and *The Museum of Americana.*

FORUGH FARROKHZAD was without a doubt one of the most significant Iranian poets of the twentieth century. Born in 1935, she was a poet of great audacity and extraordinary talent. Her poetry was the poetry of protest —protest through revelation—revelation of the innermost world of women (considered taboo until then), their intimate secrets and desires, their sorrows, longings, aspirations and at times even their articulation through silence. She died in a car crash at the age of 32. "I Will Greet the Sun Again" is from *Sin: Selected Poems of Forugh Farrokhzad,* which was awarded the Lois Roth Persian translation award in 2010.

ILMANA FASIH is a gynecologist whose passion is writing and blogging on social and health issues. An Indian married to a Pakistani, she calls herself an IndianPakistani and strives for peace between India and Pakistan. She dreams of a world without violence and wars.

CB FOLLETT, Poet Laureate of Marin County, California (2010-2013), is the author of eight poetry books and several chapbooks, most recently *Of Gravity and Tides* and *Compass Rose*. *At the Turning of the Light* won the 2001 Salmon Run National Poetry Book Award. She is editor/publisher and general dogsbody of Arctos Press and was co-editor/publisher (with Susan Terris) of *RUNES, A Review of Poetry* (2001-2008). Follett has numerous Pushcart nominations, including seven as an individual poet; a Marin Arts Council Grant for Poetry, among other awards and honors; and has been widely published.

MADELYN GARNER, co-editor of *Collecting Life: Poets on Objects Known and Imagined,* has worked as a creative writing instructor, administrator, and editor. Her awards include the Colorado Governor's Award for Excellence in the Arts and Humanities, an Aspen Writers' Conference Fellowship, the D. H. Lawrence Award, and the Jackson Hole Writers Conference Poetry Prize (2010). She has recent work in *Nimrod, Harpur Palate, Water-Stone Review, Saranac Review, PMS poemmemoirstory,* and *American Journal of Nursing,* as well as in the anthology *Beyond Forgetting: Poetry and Prose about Alzheimer's Disease.*

KATHERINE L. GORDON is a rural Ontario poet, publisher, author, reviewer, and literary critic. She believes that vibrant poetry, art, music, and the powerful spoken word will one day unite us all in peace. Her work has been published internationally and translated into several languages. Her books and anthologies may be found at the following presses: Craigleigh, Passion Among the Cacti, Hidden Brook, Serengeti, and Cyclamens and Swords.

PAT HANAHOE-DOSCH's poetry book, *Fleeing Back* (2012), was published by FutureCycle Press. Her poems have been published in *Atticus Review, Confrontation, Red River Review, San Pedro River Review, Red Ochre Lit, Nervous Breakdown, Quantum Poetry, Paterson Literary Review, Abalone Moon, Switched-on Gutenberg,* and others, and in the anthology *Paterson: The Poets' City.* Her articles have appeared in *Travel Belles, On a Junket,* and *Wholistic Living News.* Her story, "Sighting Bia," was a finalist for A Room of Her Own Foundation's 2012 Orlando Prize for Flash Fiction.

JANE HILBERRY has published a number of books, including *Body Painting* (Red Hen Press), winner of the Colorado Book Award. Her poems have appeared in *The Hudson Review, Virginia Quarterly Review,* and elsewhere. She teaches Creative Writing at Colorado College and Leadership Development at The Banff Centre in Canada.

JANE HIRSHFIELD is the author of *Come, Thief* (Knopf), a now-classic book of essays, *Nine Gates: Entering the Mind of Poetry* (HarperCollins), and six earlier award-winning poetry collections including *After* and *Given Sugar, Given Salt* (HarperCollins), a National Book Critics Circle Award finalist. She co-translated four collections of past poets' work. Awards include major fellowships from the Guggenheim and Rockefeller foundations, the National Endowment for the Arts, and the Academy of American Poets. Her work has appeared in *The New Yorker, The Atlantic, The Times Literary Supplement, Slate, Poetry,* and *The New Republic,* as well as in seven editions of *The Best American Poetry* and four Pushcart Prize anthologies. In 2012 she was elected a chancellor of the Academy of American Poets and also received the Donald Hall-Jane Kenyon Prize in American Poetry.

LINDA HOGAN, Chickasaw, is the Writer in Residence for the Chickasaw Nation. She is a writer, teacher, and activist. Her latest book is *Indios,* a long poem and performance piece. Her previous books—most of which have received awards—include the novels *The Book of Medicines, People of the Whale, Power,* and *Mean Spirit; Rounding the Human Corners* (poems); and a collection of essays, *Dwellings: A Spiritual History of the World.* A finalist for the Pulitzer Prize for Literature (1990), she was a Lannan Foundation Fellow (1994) and received Guggenheim and NEA fellowships and other awards.

PAUL HOSTOVSKY is the author of five books of poetry, most recently *Naming Names* (Main Street Rag). His poems have won a Pushcart Prize and two Best of the Net awards. He works in Boston, Massachusetts, as an Interpreter for the Deaf.

JOSEPH HUTCHISON is the author of 15 collections of poems, including *Marked Men, Thread of the Real, The Earth-Boat,* and *Bed of Coals* (winner of the 1994 Colorado Poetry Award). He makes his living as a commercial writer and as an adjunct professor of graduate-level writing and literature at the University of Denver's University College. He and his wife, yoga instructor Melody Madonna, live in the mountains southwest of Denver.

ANA ISTARÚ is an internationally recognized Costa Rican poet, playwright, newspaper columnist, and dramatic actress. She is the author of six books of poetry, among them *La estación de fiebre* (*Fever Season*, winner of the prestigious EDUCA prize for poetry), *La muerte y otros efímeros agravios* (*Death and Other Ephemeral Offenses*), and *Verbo madre* (*Mother Verb*). She has won two international awards for her plays, Spain's María Teresa de León and Hermanos Machado prizes. Her poems have been translated into many languages, including Dutch, English, French, German, and Italian.

ANITA JEPSON-GILBERT teaches ESL at the Community College of Denver. She is active in the poetry community in Colorado and helps to facilitate events for Columbine Poets.

Activist, poet, and playwright PENN KEMP (mytown.ca/pennletters) was the inaugural Poet Laureate of London, Canada. As Writer-in-Residence for Western University, her project was the DVD *Luminous Entrance: A Sound Opera for Climate Change Action* (Pendas Productions). She has published 25 books of poetry and drama. Six of her plays and ten CDs of *Sound Opera* have been produced as well as award-winning videopoems. Her latest book is *Jack Layton: Art in Action* (Quattro Books).

RITA BRADY KIEFER, once a Catholic nun, is a full-time writer in Evergreen, Colorado, where she lives with her husband, Jerry. For 20 years, she has facilitated writing sessions with domestic violence survivors. Her poetry publications include *Nesting Doll* (University Press of Colorado, a finalist for the Colorado Book Award) and two chapbooks. Her poems have been translated into Spanish, in journals in Argentina and Spain; one was the basis for a musical composition on the CD *Soundscapes* (Ars Nova). Winner of several awards for her poetry, she also has had a play produced and has completed a memoir.

DIANE KISTNER is Director, Editor/Publisher, and MHW ("Many Hat Wearer") of FutureCycle Press. A small press editor/publisher (Ali Baba Press) and prize-winning poet in the '70s, she performed her own work and published the work of other writers and artists of her day. A second edition of *Falling in Caves* (poems) came out this year. A former trauma therapist, she now devotes her talents to preserving for posterity the writings of her contemporaries. She lives in the mountains of western North Carolina with her partner, the poet Robert S. King.

DESMOND KON ZHICHENG-MINGDÉ, an interdisciplinary artist, has edited more than ten books and co-produced three audio books in the genres of ethnography, journalism, poetry, and creative nonfiction. Trained in publishing at Stanford, with a theology master's degree from Harvard and fine arts master's from Notre Dame, he is the recipient of the PEN American Center Shorts Prize, Swale Life Poetry Prize, Cyclamens and Swords Poetry Prize, and Stepping Stones Nigeria Poetry Prize, among others.

PAULA J. LAMBERT is the author of *The Sudden Seduction of Gravity* (Full/Crescent Press) and *The Guilt That Gathers* (Pudding House Press). "Anatomy of Birds, Part 1: Furcula" is from her current manuscript-in-progress, *Not All the Bones of Birds Are Hollow.* Lambert has been a resident fellow at the Virginia Center for the Creative Arts as well as an Ohio Arts Council Individual Artist Recipient. She has an MFA from Bowling Green State University.

WAYNE LEE (wayneleepoet.com) lives in Santa Fe, New Mexico. His poems have appeared in the Tupelo Press Poetry Project, *Sliver of Stone, Slipstream, The New Guard,* and other publications. Lee has been nominated for a Pushcart Prize. His third collection, *The Underside of Light,* is forthcoming from Aldrich Press.

LYN LIFSHIN (lynlifshin.com) has many books to her credit, including *Another Woman Who Looks Like Me, Barbaro: Beyond Brokenness, For the Roses: Poems After Joni Mitchell, Hitchcock Hotel, Ballroom, All the Poets Who Have Touched Me,* and *Knife Edge & Absinthe: The Tango Poems.* In Fall 2013, NYQ Books will publish *A Girl Goes into the Woods: Selected Poems.* Also forthcoming: *Secretariat: The Red Freak, The Miracle; The Tangled Alphabet: Istanbul Poems;* and *Luminous Women: Eneduhanna, Sheherazade, Nefertiti.*

BOBBI LURIE is the author of four poetry collections: *the morphine poems, Grief Suite, Letter from the Lawn,* and *The Book I Never Read.*

KEN MEISEL is a poet and psychotherapist from the Detroit area. He is a 2012 Kresge Arts Fellow, a Pushcart nominee, and the author of five poetry collections: *Beautiful Rust* (Bottom Dog Press), *Just Listening* and *Before Exiting* (Pure Heart Press), and *Sometimes the Wind* (March Street Press). His publications include *Cream City Review, Concho River Review, San Pedro River Review, Rattle, River Oak Review, Bryant Literary Review, Main Street Rag, Boxcar Review, Otis Nebula, Third Wednesday, Ruminate, Muddy River Poetry Review, The Chaffin Journal* and *Lake Effect.*

KARLA LINN MERRIFIELD (karlalinn.blogspot.com) has had 400+ poems appear in dozens of publications. Among her ten published books are her newest ones: *Lithic Scatter and Other Poems* (Mercury Heartlink) and *Attaining Canopy: Amazon Poems* (FootHills Publishing).

BASIA MILLER's poems have appeared in *Sin Fronteras, Poésie sur Seine,* and elsewhere. She has translated several bilingual limited editions of poems with art, including "Cantate pour le Grand Canyon" by Francine Caron (Transignum) and "Le Chant de Naatsis'ààn" by Marie Cayol (Imprimeries du Gard Rhodanien). With Anne Cohler and Harold Stone, she co-translated Montesquieu's *Spirit of the Laws.* She lives in Santa Fe, New Mexico.

KISHWAR NAHEED, a feminist Urdu poet from Pakistan, has written several poetry books. She also has received awards including Sitara-e-Imtiaz for her literary contribution towards Urdu literature, the Adamjee Prize of Literature for *Lab-e-goya* (1969), the UNESCO Prize for Children's Literature, the Best Translation award of Columbia University, and the Mandela Prize. "We Sinful Women" gave its title to a ground-breaking anthology of contemporary Urdu feminist poetry translated and edited by Rukhsana Ahmad, published in London by the Women's Press in 1991.

Writer, poet, former teacher, and editor RUTH OBEE (ruthobee.com) spent twenty years with her husband, a career diplomat, in South Asia and Africa. In the late 1980s, when her daughter was Malala's age, they lived in Pakistan. The Soviet-Afghanistan war was active, and later the Taliban took power. Her family experienced several dangerous situations of their own. Obee is the author of two works of non-fiction and two collections of poetry. She lives in Colorado Springs, Colorado, with her husband.

COLLEEN POWDERLY worked as a chemical dependency counselor before leaving the workforce in 2010. Poems reflecting her childhood in the deep South and youth in the Midwest formed the basis for *Split* (FootHills Publishing). More recent work has focused on stories from the working class, particularly from women's lives. Her work has appeared online in *The Centrifugal Eye* and *Sea Stories* and in many journals, including *The Palo Alto Review, RiverSedge, The Alembic, Fox Cry Review,* and *The HazMat Review.*

PEG QUINN is a two-time Pushcart Prize nominee. She paints murals and theatrical sets and teaches art at a private school in California.

CHRIS RANSICK, Denver Poet Laureate (2006-2010), is an award-winning author of five books of poetry and fiction. He has worked as a journalist, editor, professor, and speaker. His first book, *Never Summer*, won a 2003 Colorado Book Award for Poetry. All of his titles are forthcoming in new editions from Conundrum Press. He teaches at the Lighthouse Writers Workshop, Denver's preeminent independent creative writing program.

BARBARA ROCKMAN teaches poetry in Santa Fe, New Mexico. Her collection, *Sting and Nest*, received the 2012 New Mexico-Arizona Book Award and the 2012 National Press Women Book Prize. Her poems appear widely in journals and anthologies and have been recognized with the Baskerville Publisher's Prize and Southwest Writers Award.

JOAN ROBERTA RYAN is a professional writer living in Taos, New Mexico, where she indulges her lifelong passions for writing poetry, sking, hiking, and Mediterranean cooking. Her poems have appeared or are forthcoming in *The Atlanta Review, Roanoke Review, Taos Journal of Poetry and Art, Off the Coast, Concho River Review, Prick of the Spindle,* and others.

MARGE SAISER's seventh book, *Losing the Ring in the River* (University of New Mexico Press), uses persona poems to tell a story of three generations. Saiser has received an Academy of American Poets Award and the Nebraska Book Award. Her poems have been published in *The Writer's Almanac* online and in *Prairie Schooner, Field, Chattahoochee Review, Cimarron Review, Rattle,* and *Nimrod.*

AFTAB YUSUF SHAIKH is a young Indian poet based in Mumbai who has been writing since he was eight. His works have been featured in anthologies and other publications around the world including *Muse India, Istanbul Literary Review, Dance of the Peacock,* and others. He self-published his first collection, *Poems Twenty Ten.* His formal debut volume, *The Case For Sita,* is forthcoming from Virgin Leaf Books in India. He is currently pursuing a bachelor's degree in English Literature and Psychology from the University of Mumbai.

MICHAEL G. SMITH (michaelgsmithpoetry.com) has published poems in many literary journals and anthologies. He has held writing residencies at Jentel (Banner, Wyoming) and with the Spring Creek Project (Oregon State University) at Shotpouch Cabin and the H. J. Andrews Experimental Forest.

MARK SMITH-SOTO, editor of *International Poetry Review,* has published three prize-winning chapbooks and two full-length poetry books, *Our Lives Are Rivers* (University Press of Florida) and *Any Second Now* (Main Street Rag). His poetry, which won him an NEA Fellowship in 2006, has appeared in *Antioch Review, Kenyon Review, Literary Review, Nimrod, The Sun,* etc. In 2010, Unicorn Press published his translation of the selected poetry of Costa Rican writer Ana Istarú, *Fever Season.* His most recent works are *Berkeley Prelude: A Lyrical Memoir* (Unicorn Press) and *Splices* (Finishing Line Press).

MERYL STRATFORD is a retired teacher. Her poems have appeared in various magazines, and her chapbook, *The Magician's Daughter,* won the 2013 YellowJacket Press Contest. She lives in Hallandale Beach, Florida.

SHERRY STUART-BERMAN is a licensed master social worker and certified poetry therapist in training. Her poems have appeared or are forthcoming in onecityoneprompt.org, *The Paterson Literary Review, Earth's Daughters,* and *Knot.* She lives with her husband and their son in New York.

JUDITH TERZI (home.earthlink.net) wrote *Sharing Tabouli* and *The Road to Oxnard.* Recent poetry has appeared or is forthcoming in *The Centrifugal Eye*; *Myrrh, Mothwing, Smoke: Erotic Poems* (Tupelo Press); *The Raintown Review*; *Times They Were A-Changing: Women Remember the 60s & 70s* (She Writes Press); and *Ghazal for a Chambermaid* is forthcoming (Finishing Line Press). A former high school French teacher, she also taught ESL and English at California State University, Los Angeles, and in Algiers, Algeria.

ANDREA L. WATSON is founding publisher and editor of 3: A Taos Press. Her poetry has appeared in *Nimrod, Rhino, Runes, Subtropics, Ekphrasis, International Poetry Review,* and *The Dublin Quarterly,* among others. She has designed and curated sixteen ekphrasis events of poetry and art across the United States, including *Braided Lives: A Collaboration Between Artists and Poets, Interwoven Illuminations, The Sacred Blue, Reflections on RANE,* and *Fragments: Poets and Artists of the South and Southwest.* She is co-editor of *Collecting Life: Poets on Objects Known and Imagined.*

SARAH WHITE lives in New York City. For 23 years she was a Professor of French at Franklin and Marshall College in Lancaster, Pennsylvania. She is co-translator, with Matilda Bruckner and Laurie Shepard, of *Songs of the Women Troubadours* (Garland Publishing). She has published a collection of poems, *Cleopatra Haunts the Hudson* (Spuyten Duyvil), and a sequence of variations, *Alice Ages and Ages* (BlazeVox).

JOHN SIBLEY WILLIAMS is the author of six poetry chapbooks and the full-length *Controlled Hallucinations* (FutureCycle Press). A HEART Poetry Award winner, he has been a finalist for the Pushcart, Rumi, and *The Pinch* poetry prizes. He serves as editor of *The Inflectionist Review*, co-director of the Walt Whitman 150 project, and marketing director of Inkwater Press. Publishing credits include *Third Coast, Nimrod, Inkwell, Cider Press Review, Bryant Literary Review, Cream City Review, The Chaffin Journal, The Evansville Review, RHINO,* etc., and various anthologies. He lives in Portland, Oregon.

KATHRYN WINOGRAD, poet and essayist, is on the English and creative writing faculty for Arapahoe Community College and on the poetry faculty for Ashland University's low residency MFA program. She won the Colorado Book Award for Poetry for *Air Into Breath* (Ashland Poetry Press) and was first-place winner in the Non-rhyming Poetry category of the *Writer's Digest* 80th Annual Writing Competition. A creative nonfiction essay collection, *Phantom Canyon,* is forthcoming from Conundrum Press.

SHOLEH WOLPÉ was born in Iran. She spent most of her teen years in Trinidad and the United Kingdom before settling in the United States. Sholeh is a recipient of 2013 Midwest Book Award and 2010 Lois Roth Persian Translation prize. Her eight publications include three collections of poetry, three anthologies, and two books of translations. Her most recent publications are *Keeping Time with Blue Hyacinths* and *Breaking the Jaws of Silence: Sixty American Poets Speak to the World.*

DIANA WOODCOCK's first full-length poetry collection, *Swaying on the Elephant's Shoulders,* won the 2010 Vernice Quebodeaux International Poetry Prize (Little Red Tree Publishing). Her chapbooks are *In the Shade of the Sidra Tree, Mandala,* and *Travels of a Gwai Lo* (the title poem of which was nominated for a Pushcart Prize). Her fourth chapbook, *Tamed by the Desert,* is forthcoming from Finishing Line Press. Currently teaching at Virginia Commonwealth University in Qatar, she has worked in Tibet, Macau, and Thailand.

ABIGAIL WYATT was born in Essex but long ago made her home in Cornwall. She began writing seriously in 2007 and, since then, her work has appeared in more than seventy magazines and journals. She is the joint editor of *Murder of Krows* (I & II), which features the work of emerging poets living in Cornwall, as well as an editor of *Poetry24.* She most recently published *Old Soldiers, Old Bones and Other Stories* in conjunction with Simon Million of One Million Stories.

VASSILIS ZAMBARAS, born in Greece, returned there after 25 years in the United States. He is semi-retired from teaching ESL at the language school he founded in 1977 in Meligalas. He has published two small poetry books, *Sentences* (Querencia) and *Aural* (Singing Horse), and a foldout booklet of poems, *In Credible Evidence* (Longhouse). His work appears in *How the Net Is Gripped: A Selection of Contemporary American Poetry* (Stride) and in *Poetry Salzburg Review, The London Magazine, First Intensity, Arabesques Review, Shearsman, Poetry Northwest, The Salt River Review,* and others.

Acknowledgments

Carol Alena Aronoff, "Letter to the Parents of Prospective Suicide Bombers," first appeared in a different form in *Her Soup Made the Moon Weep* by Carol Alena Aronoff (Pelican Pond, 2007).

Ellen Bass, "Bearing Witness," is from *Mules of Love*. Copyright © 2002 by Ellen Bass. Reprinted with the permission of The Permissions Company, Inc., on behalf of BOA Editions Ltd., www.boaeditions.org.

April Bulmer, "Dove Tale," first appeared online in *The 6S Network: What Can You Say in Six Sentences?*

Conrad DiDiodato, "Malala," first appeared online in *Word-Dreamer: poetics.*

Forugh Farrokhzad, "I Will Greet the Sun Again," translated by Sholeh Wolpé, is from *Sin: Selected Poems of Forugh Farrokhzad*. Copyright © 2007 by Sholeh Wolpé. Reprinted with the permission of The Permissions Company, Inc., on behalf of the University of Arkansas Press, www.uapress.com.

CB Follett, "Horses of Pain," first appeared in *One Bird Falling* by CB Follett (Time Being Books, 2011).

Jane Hilberry, "In Arabic," first appeared in *Body Painting* by Jane Hilberry (Red Hen Press, 2005).

Jane Hirshfield, "Like the Small Hole by the Path-Side Something Lives In," first appeared in *Poetry.*

Joseph Hutchison, "Malala," first appeared online in *The Perpetual Bird.*

Diane Kistner, "The Lamps of Night," first appeared in *The Sun.*

Desmond Kon Zhicheng-Mingdé, "Grenouille Bleue," winner of the Naani Poetry Prize, first appeared in *Vallum.*

Wayne Lee, "Song for Rahim Alhaj," first appeared in *Aunt Chloe.*

Bobbie Lurie, "Kabul," first appeared in *The Book I Never Read* by Bobbie Lurie (WordTech Communications, 2003).

Kishwar Nheed, "We Sinful Women," translated by Rukhsana Ahmad, first appeared in *Tablet & Pen: Literary Landscapes from the Modern Middle East*, ed. Reza Aslan (W. W. Norton & Co., 2010).

Peg Quinn, "Note to Taliban," first appeared online in *New Verse News*.

Chris Ransick, "Ghazal for a Murdered Poet," first appeared in *Lost Songs & Last Chances* by Chris Ransick (Ghost Road Press, 2006).

Marge Saiser, "I Have Nothing to Say about Fire," first appeared in *Losing the Ring in the River* by Marge Saiser (University of New Mexico Press, 2013).

Meryl Stratford, "How the Night Fish Live," first appeared, in a slightly different version, as "Diving into the Wreck" in *Adrienne Rich: A Tribute Anthology* (Split Oak Press, 2012).

Andrea L. Watson, "All the Ways You Know to Love Us," first appeared in *Borderlands: Texas Poetry Review*.

Sholeh Wolpé, "Pickles and Donuts" and "The Rosetta Stone," first appeared in *Keeping Time with Blue Hyacinths* by Sholeh Wolpé (University of Arkansas Press, 2013).

Abigail Wyatt, "Holy Housework," originally titled "Holy Housework or a Fresh Start," first appeared in *Poetry24*.

Cover art, "Covering the Sun," by Laura Eklund (lauraeklund.org); cover and book design by Diane Kistner (dkistner@futurecycle.org); Adobe Garamond Pro text and titling with author names set in Tork

About FutureCycle Press

FutureCycle Press is dedicated to publishing lasting English-language poetry and flash fiction books, chapbooks, and anthologies in both print-on-demand and ebook formats. Founded in 2007 by long-time independent editor/publishers and partners Diane Kistner and Robert S. King, the press incorporated as a nonprofit in 2012. A number of our editors are distinguished poets and writers in their own right, and we have been involved in the small press movement going back to the early seventies.

The FutureCycle Poetry Book Prize and honorarium is awarded annually for the best full-length volume of poetry we publish in a calendar year. Introduced in 2013, our Good Works projects are devoted to issues of global significance, with all proceeds donated to a related worthy cause. We are dedicated to giving all authors we publish the care their work deserves, making our catalog of titles the most distinguished it can be, and paying forward any earnings to fund more great books.

We've learned a few things about independent publishing over the years. We've also evolved a unique, resilient publishing model that allows us to focus mainly on vetting and preserving for posterity the most books of exceptional quality without becoming overwhelmed with bookkeeping and mailing, fundraising, or taxing editorial and production "bubbles." To find out more about what we are doing, come see us at www.futurecycle.org.

FutureCycle Good Works

Good Works projects are issue-oriented anthologies of work designed to increase awareness and help make our world a better place. These projects provide an organized way for poets and writers to contribute to causes they write, and care, about. Each anthology is published on our website in PDF format for free download and sharing; paperback and Kindle ebook editions go on sale globally to benefit a related worthy cause.

Sales of the anthology *American Society: What Poets See,* edited by David Chorlton and Robert S. King, help fund the core Good Works operations. Specific project sales are designated for donation to a cause related to the theme of the project. (For example, our first Good Works project, *Malala: Poems for Malala Yousafzai,* benefits the Malala Fund.) Open projects and submission link/deadlines are listed on the Good Works tab at www.futurecycle.org, along with links to the PDFs when published.

Made in the USA
Charleston, SC
01 August 2014